queens of STEAM

Mary Oliver

The Art and Life of A Prized American Poet

by Mari Bolte

Copyright © 2023 by Paw Prints Publishing

Image credits: Cover: Kevork Djansezian/Getty Images; 3: Kevork Djansezian/ Getty Images; 4: Daniel Chester French/Wikimedia; 5: Frederick M. Brown/ Getty Images, Clker-Free-Vector-Images/Pixabay; 6: Jose Luis Stephens/ Shutterstock; 7: ArtsyBee/Pixabay, katarinag/Shutterstock; 8: J. W. Rochlitz/ Wikimedia, Osama Shukir Muhammed Amin FRCP(Glasg)/Wikimedia; 9: PhotoQuest/Getty Images; 10: Jon Bilous/Shutterstock; 11: David Bokuchava/Shutterstock; 12: Robin Marchant/Getty Images; 13: lunamarina/ Shutterstock; 14: ArtsyBee/Pixabay, Marc Espolet/Getty Images, Mary Anne Love/Shutterstock; 15: Yurii Zymovin/Shutterstock; 16: Sudowood/Getty Images; 17: alexkich/Getty Images; 18: Museum of the City of New York/ Getty Images; 20: everst/Shutterstock; 21: Mary Anne Love/Shutterstock; 22; Kevork Djansezian/Getty Images; 23: Net Vector/Shutterstock; 25: Sepp photography/Shutterstock; 26: Dave Kotinsky/Getty Images, Martin Godwin/ Getty Images, GraphicaArtis/Getty Images, Roger Kisby/Getty Images, Hindustan Times/Getty Images; background: incomible/Getty Images

9781223187402 English Hardcover
9781223187419 English Paperback
9781223187426 English eBook

Published by Paw Prints Publishing
PawPrintsPublishing.com
Printed in China

See the Glossary on page 29 for definitions of words found in **bold** in the text!

“Whoever you are, no matter how lonely, the world offers itself to your imagination.”

–Mary Oliver

A Humble "Queen"

It's a spring day in 1984, and Mary Oliver is taking a walk. This is not unusual. Mary takes a walk every day. Usually in the woods. This is where she writes.

But Mary's not in the woods at the moment. She's not writing. She's at the town dump! There, she hopes to find shingles to fix the roof of her house.

No one would ever suspect that, just that morning, this humble poet had learned she'd won a special award. Her book, *American **Primitive**,* had been given the Pulitzer Prize for Poetry.

The Pulitzer Prize is an annual award. Writers, journalists, and musicians are recognized for their work in over 20 different categories.

Mary is one of America's most beloved poets. She is a master of the art form. Some may even say a "Queen."

Mary grew up on the edge of a big city, Cleveland, Ohio.

Lonely Kingdom

Before she walked the woods (or town dump!) of Provincetown, Massachusetts, Mary explored the nature around her childhood home near Cleveland, Ohio. She was born on September 10, 1935. Her early life was lonely. Her family life was unloving. She found peace in the **enchantment** of the woods around her.

Many people find peace in nature.

In the woods, Mary built huts out of sticks and grass. She would rest in them and read books like those by Walt Whitman to keep her mind busy. Walt Whitman's poetry about nature spoke to Mary. She began to write her own nature poetry. "I made a world out of words," she later said.

During these moments, a "queen" was born.

Walt Whitman was a poet and essayist in the 1800s. He wrote of nature and human relationships.

Poetry is one of the oldest forms of human art. *The Epic of Gilgamesh* is the oldest epic poem. It dates back to 2100 BCE*.

*Before Common Era (BCE) is before year 1

Mary would grow to admire many more poets as she got older. The poet Edna St. Vincent Millay became her hero. Edna passed away in 1950. Mary never got to meet her. But she did befriend Edna's sister and helped her organize Edna's home after the poet died. The home, Steepletop, was in New York State. Looking through Edna's work at Steepletop was life-changing for a 17-year-old Mary. Even after later moving to New York City, she would return to Steepletop many times for inspiration.

Edna St. Vincent Millay

Edna St. Vincent Millay (1892–1950) was a "Queen of **STEAM**" in her own right. She was the first woman to win the Pulitzer Prize for Poetry. Her poems spoke of youthful **rebellion** and independence. She wasn't afraid to write about women's issues and politics. Like Mary Oliver, she wrote about the wild. In many ways, Edna passed her royal crown on to Mary.

In 1959, during one of her visits to Steepletop, Mary was introduced to another house guest randomly one evening. When they first met, Mary and this stranger—Molly Malone Cook— immediately locked eyes. It was love at first sight. Most of Mary's poems after this were dedicated to Molly.

Molly was a photographer. The two moved to Provincetown, Massachusetts, in 1964, and they lived there together for the rest of their lives.

Provincetown has attracted writers and artists since the 1870s. The first art **colony** was opened there in 1899. By 1916, it was the biggest art colony in the world.

Gathering food from the wild is called foraging.

Mary would get up every morning at 5 a.m. to explore the Province Lands National Seashore. This 3,500-acre park is full of forests and ponds.

When Mary went on her "writing walks," she would also gather food like berries, clams, and mushrooms. She'd bring this food back home for her and Molly to eat.

The Beginning of an Empire

Mary and Molly opened a bookstore in Provincetown. They filled it with books, as well as sass and attitude, often jesting with their customers for fun. Artist John Waters worked there before he was famous. He got to know Mary well. "[Mary] was funny and lovely," he later said. But she also had another side. People who only knew her as a quirky woman in the woods never saw it. "She was a drama queen," John laughed.

John Waters is a filmmaker, actor, artist, and writer. He has been nominated for two **Grammy** Awards.

Provincetown is a popular place for tourists. It is located
at the end of Cape Cod in the state of Massachusetts.

Mary's first book of poetry, *No Voyage and Other Poems,* was published in 1963. She was 28. The poems were about nature and how people, animals, and plants **coexist**. Her words reminded readers to **cherish** moments in nature. Whether they were ordinary happenings or extraordinary occurrences, miracles were always present.

Five Mary Oliver Poems Everyone Should Read

Mary stored pencils in trees. If she was inspired while on a walk, she could write down her thoughts immediately. She never walked with a destination in mind. If she stopped to write, it was a successful walk. Here are five essential poems to experience this "nature queen's" work:

1. "Wild Geese"
2. "A Dream of Trees"
3. "The Summer Day"
4. "The Swan"
5. "The Journey"

Mary lived a **reclusive** life. She ruled the forest, not the people. Many writers who find fame often teach or travel. But Mary chose to spend time at home. She and Molly were together nearly every day. It was a simple life.

Nature writing can include poetry, essays, and even travel and adventure stories.

Mary kept writing, and her next book came out in 1972. It was a collection of poems called *The River Styx, Ohio, and Other Poems*. Mary put out a new book every year or two after that. Over her career, she published more than 25 books!

Poetry for the Mind

Some people read Mary's poems every day as a form of **meditation**. Read some of Mary's words below, and then take a few minutes to consider what they mean.

- *Mindful*: "Every day I see or I hear something that more or less kills me with delight."
- *On Meditating Sort Of*: "Some days I fall asleep, or land in that even better place—half asleep—where the world, spring, summer, autumn, winter—flies through my mind in its hardy **ascent** and its uncompromising **descent**."
- *Snow Geese*: "Oh, to love what is lovely, and will not last!"

Mary never looked back for inspiration. Like one of her walks through the woods, the only direction was forward. She was just as confident about *how* she wrote. Her poetry was **succinct** and easy to understand. Every word was necessary.

Joseph Pulitzer, a newspaper publisher,
started the Pulitzer Prize.

The Crown Jewel of Awards

In 1983, *American Primitive* was published. It was Mary's fifth book. She was still not very well-known at the time. Then, the book won the Pulitzer Prize and people began to ask, "Who's Mary Oliver?" Mary had never given readings or interviews. As a child, she tried hard not to be noticed. She carried this desire her entire life. After the award, she chose to stay behind her "castle walls."

DID YOU KNOW?! There are writing contests just for kids! Like this one: Every year, EngineerGirl asks students to write an essay about how female and/or BIPOC engineers contribute to STEAM.

Mary's book *New and Selected Poems* won the National Book Award in 1992. This award is given to the best literature in the United States each year. In her acceptance speech, Mary thanked Molly, "the best reader anybody could ever have. She is the light of my life, and I'd like to thank her publicly."

Mary Oliver, Overlooked

Although Mary received rewards, her work was often overlooked. Some critics said it lacked **sophistication**. They said that writing about nature and beauty was old-fashioned. Because people used it as inspiration for meditation or yoga, it seemed simple. Mary didn't listen. She didn't change the way she wrote or what she wrote about. The only person Mary had to prove something to was herself.

MARY OLIVER · A THOUSAND MORNINGS

MARY OLIVER WILD GEESE — BLOODAXE WORLD POETS

Mary Oliver — A Poetry Handbook — Harcourt

Oliver — TWELVE MOONS

AMERICAN PRIMITIVE — MARY OLIVER

Mary Oliver — west wind — MARINER BOOKS

White Pine — Harcourt

MARY OLIVER | BLUE HORSES — Penguin Press

MARY OLIVER — THIRST — BEACON PRESS

EVIDENCE — POEMS BY MARY OLIVER — BEACON PRESS

Mary Oliver — Blue Pastures — HARCOURT BRACE

MARY OLIVER NEW AND SELECTED POEMS — VOLUME ONE — BEACON

MARY OLIVER NEW AND SELECTED POEMS — VOLUME TWO — BEACON

Mary published essays as well as poems. One of her most popular is called "My Friend Walt Whitman."

Mary's poems were then published in magazines around the country. She became one of the best-selling poets in America. She **reigned** over booklists, joining nobility like Rod McKuen, Jalal al-Din Rumi, and William Shakespeare. By the mid-2000s, there would be more than half a million copies of her work in print.

Mary lost Molly to lung cancer in 2005. During her lifetime, Molly refused to publish her photographs in a book. So Mary did it for her after she died. Mary's writings and Molly's pictures merged in a book called *Our World*.

Mary read her poem "The Journey" at the 2010 Women's Conference in California.

At this point, Mary decided she was ready to meet her public. She began making more appearances. In 2005, she announced she would visit Seattle, and tickets for the 900-seat hall sold out in just a week. Hundreds of people bought books. Three years later, she returned. This time, she was at a much larger venue. Still, all 2,700 seats were snatched up in record time.

Mary **narrated** some of her books on tape. She believed poetry should be read and heard.

A Kingdom of Amazement

Loving the planet was one of Mary's favorite subjects. Her later work explored how climate change was affecting Earth. Mary reminded readers that our lives and our planet are intertwined.

Reasonable Words

Research has found that poetry can help make the urgency of climate change more real for people. The idea of climate change can cause fear, anxiety, or even denial. Poetry can educate by using straightforward language that anyone can understand. It can also help turn negative emotions into positive action for change.

Intense human activity for the past 200 years is driving climate change.

Five Female Poets to Read Next

1. **Maya Angelou**: A civil rights activist, Maya wrote about her life and struggles as a Black woman.

2. **Sappho**: Sappho's poetry about women and their relationships has been admired since her time in ancient Greece.

3. **Kimiko Hahn**: Kimiko is inspired by classic women poets in Asia as she writes about Asian American identity.

4. **Amanda Gorman**: The first US National Youth Poet Laureate, Amanda writes about issues pertaining to women, minorities, and the planet.

5. **Rupi Kaur**: This Indian-born poet writes about peace and strength when faced with heartbreak and tragedy.

In 2012, Mary was **diagnosed** with lung cancer. She didn't really speak about it, but she did write four poems about what she called "the cancer visit." Death had "left his calling card," she wrote. She was given a clean bill of health after treatment. But it didn't last.

Mary died from cancer on January 17, 2019, at age 83. Her final book was *Devotions*, a compilation of poetry from her 50-year career that she created herself. She included a reprint of her poem, "When Death Comes." It talks about embracing life and every moment.

Like any noble queen, Mary Oliver left behind a legacy.

> *When it's over, I want to say all my life*
>
> *I was a bride married to amazement.*
>
> *I was the bridegroom, taking the world into my arms.*

Quiz

1. Mary's favorite park to visit was:
   A. Central Park

   B. Yosemite National Park

   C. Province Lands National Seashore

   D. Provincetown Park

2. Mary's first published work came out in:
   A. 1963

   B. 1984

   C. 1935

   D. 1959

3. Poetry and climate change work together to:
   A. help curb carbon emissions

   B. create a desire for change

   C. speak up for animals who can't speak for themselves

   D. create a catchy tune that people can easily remember

4. Mary and Molly opened a:
   A. bookstore

   B. art gallery

   C. warehouse

   D. restaurant

Key: 1) C; 2) A; 3) B; 4) A

Glossary

ascent (uh-SENT): the act of moving upward

cherish (CHEHR-uhsh): to appreciate and love something

coexist (koh-uhg-ZIST): to live at the same time without having problems

colony (KAH-luh-nee): a group of people living together, separate from main society

descent (di-SENT): the act of moving downward

diagnosed (dai-uhg-NOHST): to have a doctor officially say you have a specific illness

enchantment (en-CHANT-muhnt): having a feeling of magic and beauty

Grammy (GRAHM-ee): an award given for accomplishments in music

meditation (meh-duh-TAY-shun): the practice of quieting one's body and mind

narrated (NEHR-ay-tuhd): to be read out loud

primitive (PRIM-uh-tiv): having to do with the ancient past

rebellion (ruh-BEL-yuhn): an effort to resist against authority

reclusive (ruh-KLOO-suhv): living alone

reigned (RAYND): ruled as a king or queen

sophistication (suh-fih-stuh-KAY-shun): highly developed and experienced

STEAM (STEEM): the fields of Science, Technology, Engineering, Arts, and Mathematics; writing and poetry are part of the arts

succinct (suh-SINGKT): using few words

ACTIVITY

Poems in Peace

Partner up with an adult in your life and choose a Mary Oliver poem to read together. Revisit page 17 for ideas or search your library or online. Print it out or copy it down. Pack a pencil and a small notebook, too. Then, take a walk together and find somewhere quiet and peaceful to sit—preferably outdoors! You should be comfortable and relaxed.

Read the poem you picked out loud. Then, close your eyes. Think about what you just read. Did any part of the poem stand out to you? What do you think Mary was writing about? Does it remind you of anything? Ask your partner the same.

Write down any words, emotions, or ideas that come to you as you meditate. Then, use what you wrote down as inspiration to write your own poem. Share the poems with one another.

And then, for good measure, hide a pencil wherever you are! For "Queen Mary"!

Descriptive Poetry

Words are how we bring things to life for others. Pick a topic—it can be anything! Will it be your favorite person, place, or thing? Or will it be something less serious, like your sibling's appearance when they wake up in the morning or something funny you saw on TV?

First, make a list of words you think of when you imagine your subject. Don't think—just write down the first things that pop into your head. "Warm," "noisy," "disruptive," "cozy," and "jealous" could be examples.

Then, make a list of more descriptive words about your subject. Use all your senses. Describe its look, feel, smell, taste, and sound. Maybe your brother's hair looks like a fuzzy spider first thing in the morning. Maybe your sister's snores sound like an airplane taking off.

How do these descriptions make you feel? Happy? Sad? Silly? Tired?

Now you can start writing your poem! Use the ideas and examples you wrote down to bring your subject to life.

Index